Stretto House

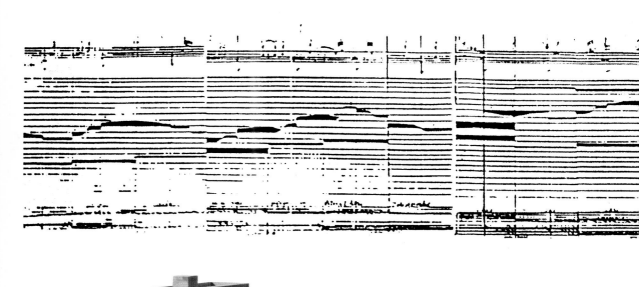

Stretto House

Steven Holl Architects

Introduction by Steven Holl

THE MONACELLI PRESS

Architect	Steven Holl Architects, New York
Principal	Steven Holl
Project Architect	Adam Yarinsky
Project Team	Peter Lynch, Bryan Bell, Matthew Karlen,
	William Wilson, Stephen Cassell, Kent Hikida,
	Florian Schmidt, Thomas Jenkinson, Lucinda Knox
Consulting Architect	Max Levy, Dallas
Landscape Consultant	Kings Creek Landscaping
Structural Consultant	Datum Engineering
Mechanical Consultant	Interfield Engineering
Contractor	Thomas S. Byrne Construction

First published in the United States of America in 1996 by
The Monacelli Press, Inc.,
10 East 92nd Street, New York, New York 10128.

Library of Congress Cataloging-in-Publication Data
Stretto House : Steven Holl Architects / introduction by Steven Holl.
p. cm. — (One house)
Includes bibliographical references.
ISBN 1-885254-29-6 (pbk.)
1. Stretto House (Dallas, Tex.) 2. Architecture, Postmodern—Texas—Dallas.
3. Steven Holl Architects. 4. Dallas (Tex.)—Buildings, structures, etc. I. Holl, Steven.
II. Steven Holl Architects. III. Series.
NA7238.D2S76   1996
728'.372'097642812—dc20   96-5621

Printed and bound in Italy

Designed and composed by *Group* C Inc New Haven/Boston

Stretto Contents

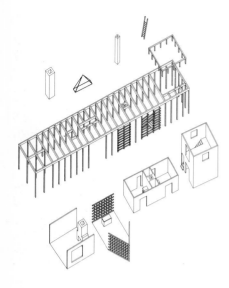

Space brings the acoustic near to life.
—John Cage

The concept for our Martha's Vineyard house of 1986 was based on a reading of Herman Melville's *Moby-Dick* and the connection to the whale skeleton, which led to a bonelike, linear structure. The native American literary space inspired the creation of an exoskeleton form given materiality in wood construction. The wood structural frame was pulled outside the normal building envelope; large four-by-six timbers were notched into six-by-ten beams in a way that drew a "ribcage" around the building. The conceptual nexus—novel, bone, whale skeleton—was given physical expression in the materiality of this wood frame, which was then bleached so that it comes even closer to a kind of boniness. The exposed frame's linearity and its linear shadows become entangled with the linear vegetation on the delicate sand dunes.

A similar consideration of materials always enters our design process from the very beginning. Even before the idea has been settled upon, we work on various models in different materials. Using little sticks to make a model results in a linear composition that might be related to wood construction. The use of chipboard results in a planar model. Clay can make a volumetric free-form. Wire leads to structures in suspension, tensile tectonics. Cast plaster suggests cast concrete and the plastic capabilities of the material. In building these sketch models, a direction is already beginning in the project. In other words, the conceptual process or idea—sketching, making watercolors, writing down sentences—is formed simultaneously with this material exploration. It is important that they run parallel.

From the start of the project, the Stretto House was rather ideal. One of the clients (who prefer to remain anonymous) had grown up in a Frank Lloyd Wright house and had a family history of appreciation of fine architecture. The joy that carefully proportioned space, inspired use of light, and thoughtful details can bring to day-to-day life had already been established as a requirement when the clients began to interview architects. They saw many of our projects in our exhibition at the Museum of Modern Art in March 1989, which helped to finalize their choice.

On the first visit to the site (after studying the written program), I suggested that the chosen one on Turtle Creek in Dallas was too small. We visited other options the next day and discovered the final site, which was occupied by a shabby wood-frame house (later removed). The site was then "recycled," and much of the existing landscape was retained, including a stream with three concrete dams and ponds, which created the constant sound of water overlapping.

In the initial sketches, we looked at the Texas vernacular materials of concrete block and metal roofs. The need for shade from the hot Texas sun provoked explorations of shadow and overlap in the sketches. After discussions with one of my former students, John Szto, a pianist from the Juilliard music school, I decided to explore the musical concept of "stretto," which is analogous to the site's overlapping ponds. In a fugue stretto, the imitation of the subject in close succession is answered before it is completed. This dovetailing musical concept could, I imagined, be an idea for a fluid connection of architectural spaces.

A particular piece of music was chosen for its extensive use of stretto—Béla Bartók's *Music for Strings, Percussion, and Celeste*. In four movements, the piece has distinct division between heavy (percussion) and light (strings). Where music has a materiality in instrumentation and sound this architecture attempts an analog in light and space.

Like the score, the building has four sections, each consisting of two modes: heavy orthogonal masonry and light curvilinear metal. The metal roofs overlap masonry "spatial dams." In the main house, "aqueous space" is developed by several means: floor planes pull the level of one space through to the next, roof planes pull space over walls, and an arched wall pulls light down from a skylight. Materials—poured concrete, glass cast in fluid shapes, slumped glass, and liquid terrazzo—and details continue the spatial concepts. The plan is purely orthogonal, while the section is curvilinear. The guest house is an inversion with the plan curvilinear and the section orthogonal, similar to the inversions of the subject in the first movement of the Bartók score.

$$\frac{\text{material x sound}}{\text{time}} = \frac{\text{material x light}}{\text{space}}$$

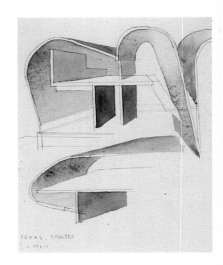

Arriving at the house via a driveway bridging the stream, visitors enter at a stone courtyard with a "melting ice" fountain. A view through the main entry reveals the overlapping spaces of the house, with glimpses of the flanking gardens along the perspective of the major rooms (which were required for a large art collection). A gradual fluid movement descends through the spatial dams, propelled by the curving roofs. Although the heavy and light contrasts in the house are clearly articulated on the exterior with masonry and metal, in the interior a more fluid continuity is achieved by slightly revealing the method of construction in material and details. The flowing spatial sequence was designed in a series of interior overlapping perspectives. The proportions were fine-tuned according to the Golden Section ratio of 1:1.618. (It is no coincidence that Bartók composed according to the Golden Section.)

The perspective of overlapping thin roofs finally opens out over the pool court as parasol-like shading. The last room in the sequence is empty and flooded by the ponds—a flooded room without pragmatic function. This flooded room, doubled by its reflection, becomes the center of two sequences of space, one from the landscape and site, the other from the aqueous space of the architecture.

The materials and method of construction follow the heavy/light and orthogonal/curved rhythm of the concept. The spatial dams are ground-face concrete block in double-wall construction; when extra strength was needed, a column was poured into the cavity. The design of the roofs was more challenging, as they curve freely in several directions. We made a model and mocked up a full-size coping edge in our office. We decided that we wanted a roof no thicker than about seven inches, to achieve the heavy-to-light rhythm. Working with Thomas Taylor of Datum Engineering in Dallas, we investigated poured-concrete shells or steel beams, construction systems either too thick or too expensive. Finally we settled on standard six-inch steel pipes bent by computer-driven magnetic-induction technology. Whenever a long span occurred, the wall thickness of the pipe was increased internally so that none of the final roofs were thicker than the overall seven-inch profile. After bending, the pipes—like large steel noodles—were numbered and delivered to the site. They were erected and field-welded with fish-mouth joints in an astonishingly rapid time. The "noodles" were braced in steel pockets in the masonry walls—thus the heavy/light and orthogonal/curved concept became a construction essence.

The details of the house were handled with special care by Thomas S. Byrne Construction (builders of Louis Kahn's Kimbell Art Museum in Fort Worth). Exterior materials of hand-sanded aluminum and acid-reddened brass yield an organic patina on the metallic areas which balances the concrete block trimmed in natural Texas limestone.

Specially woven wool carpets depict musical scores floating like rafts on the integrally colored glossy black concrete floors. Several curved-glass light fixtures were individually designed to demark particular areas in the house. In the kitchen area, the heavy/light and orthogonal/curved concept is again recalled in the wire pulls of the cabinetry.

From initial concept to finest detail, our aim is for idea and phenomena. An overall idea is like a chain of causes and effects working with functions and physical elements. Unlike a beginning in form, the concept transcends the abstract, organizing the experiential phenomena. The pleasure of architectural experiences—the phenomena of light and spatial sequence, textures, smells and sounds—is irreducible and ultimately enmeshed with situation, season, and time of day. In a way, the concept that drives a design like the Stretto House disappears completely in the phenomena of the physical reality and yet intuitively the abundance of the idea may be felt.

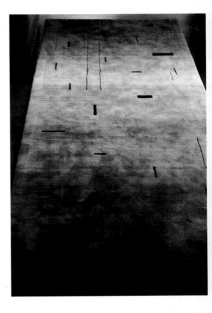

I believe the concept should be equal to that of planting a seed in which the concept—that is, the result you are going to get—should be quite clear. As you progress and develop, the form will be modified, and you should welcome this, because the concept will be so strong that you cannot destroy it.
        —Louis Kahn

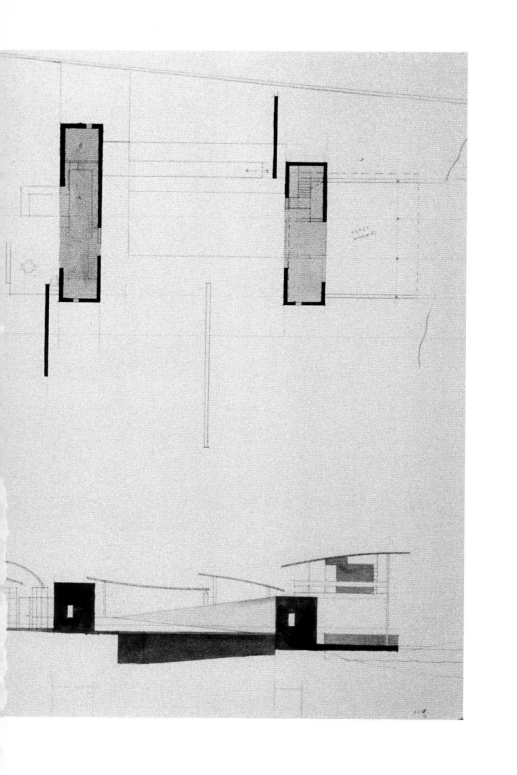

concept watercolor: house divided into four measures alternating heavy and light

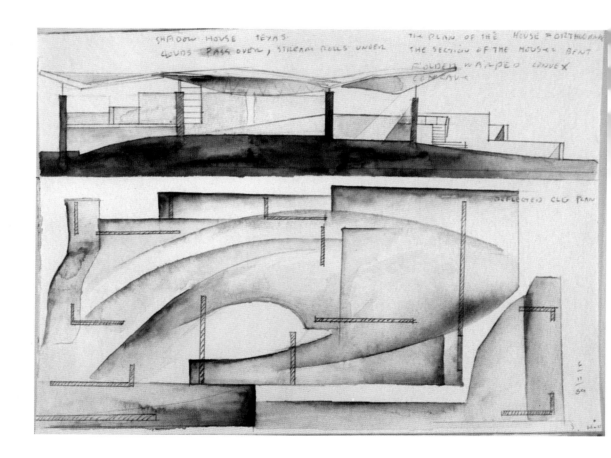

early watercolor: shadows and fluid space

early watercolor: metal roofs and masonry

early watercolor: Texas vernacular

TEXAS STRETTO

S. HOLL

early watercolor: stretto, or overlap

site plan

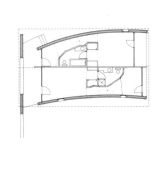

guest house (plan, elevations, section), which forms a screen in front of main house

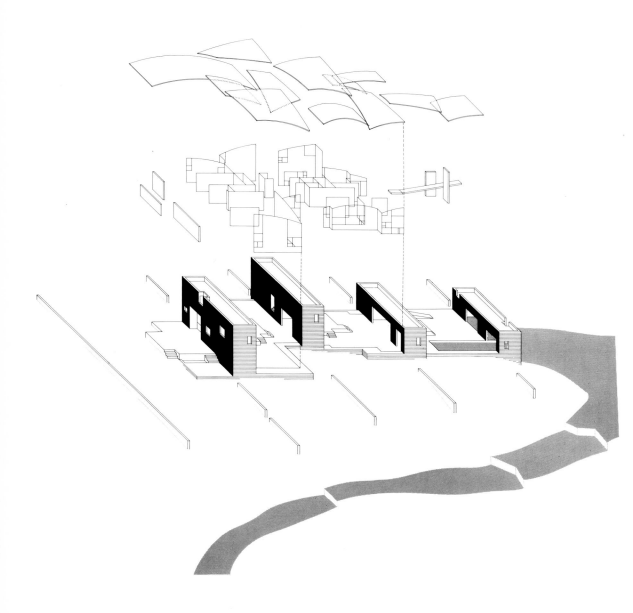

exploded axonometric showing aqueous space and spatial dams

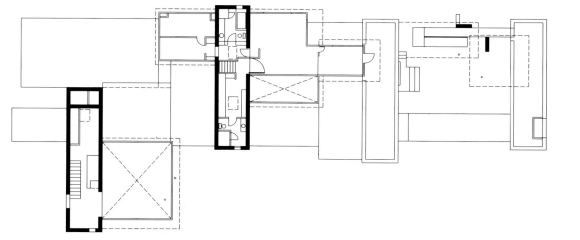

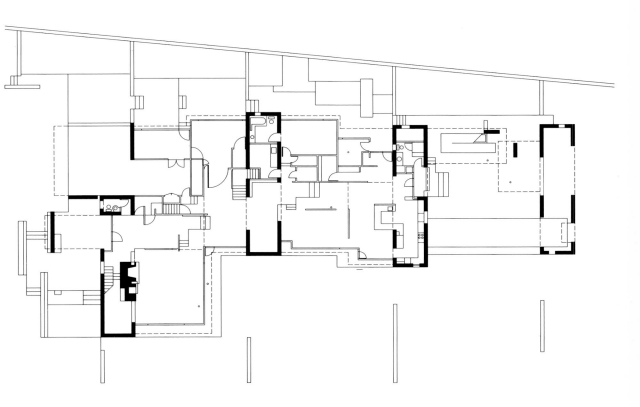

upper level (top) and main level plans

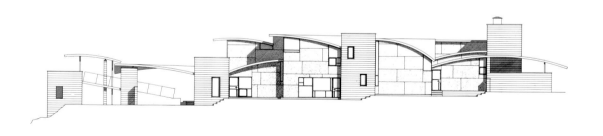

east (top) and west elevations

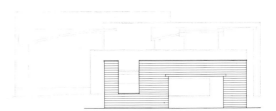

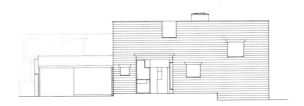

north (top) and south elevations

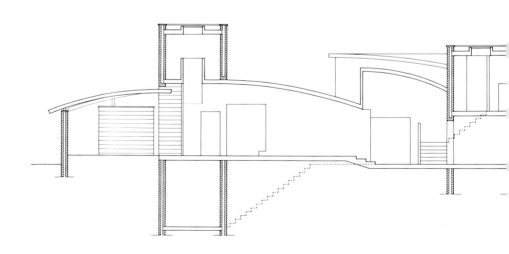

sections

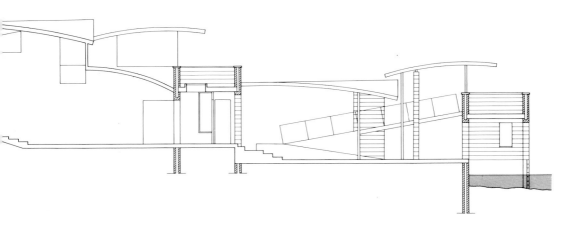

final watercolor: pool court

final watercolors: view from entry toward rear of house (top) and living room

1 south facade from entry court (preceding pages)

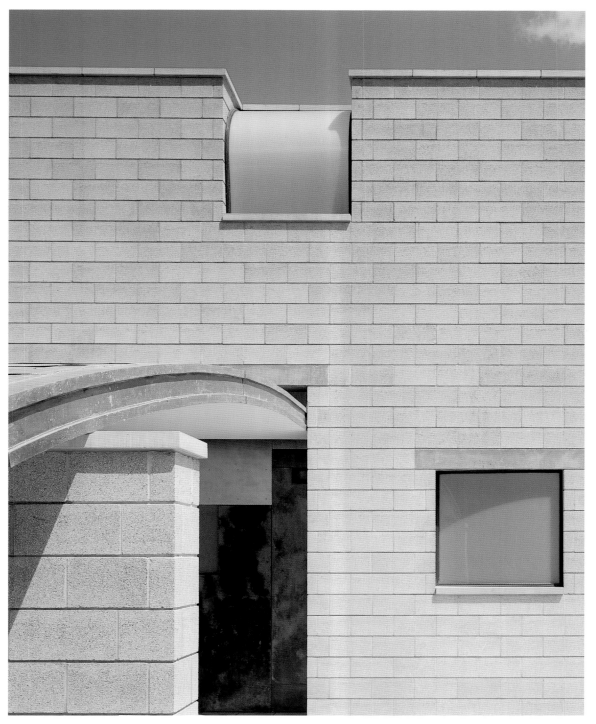

2 entry porch

3 main entry **4** cast-bronze handle on entry door

5 entry court and cast-glass fountain from entry area
6 "melting ice" fountain

7 entry area with cast-glass inserts

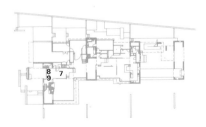

8 detail of entry-area ceiling **9** reddened brass mat in entry area

10 view showing living room (at left, with Bruce Nauman sculpture) and entry area

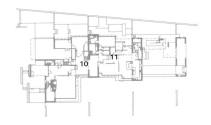

11 view toward entry area from rear of house

12 stair from entry area to art library
13 view along stair toward main entry

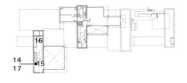

14 main entry from stair landing   **15** balcony off stair landing overlooking living room
16 curved art library window   **17** bronze rail

18
19

18 living-room balcony

19 view from balcony through living-room window, showing aqueous space and spatial dams

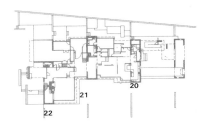

20 lead-coated copper roofs over steel tubes,
    which were computer bent by magnetic induction (preceding pages)
21 view into living room **22** view past living room toward flooded room

23 living room with fireplace, passageway to stair, and balcony
24 view from passageway to stair through living room toward library

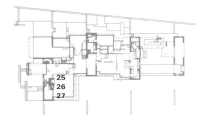

25 silver-leaf Counterpoint Table 26 wooden Quarter-Note Table

27 wooden Half-Note Table on Score Carpet in living room

28 view from balcony across living room toward upper-level stair
29 door to room for Robert Irwin's *Disk*

30 A, B, C, D light studies in *Disk* room

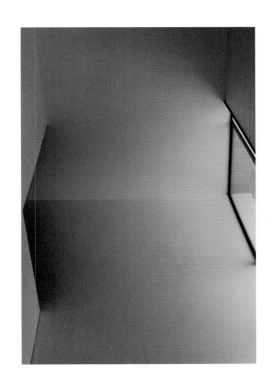

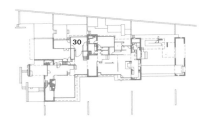

31 hanging roof over *Disk* room

32 hanging roof from *Disk* room

33 upper-level stair and entrance to library

34 view toward rear of house with Score Carpet in foreground and dining room on right

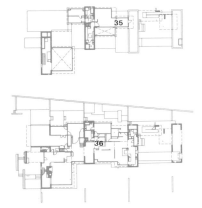

35 view of master bedroom toward terrace with balcony (at right)
36 view toward rear of house with master-bedroom balcony above

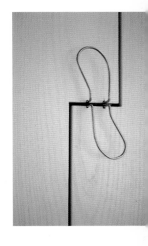

37, 38 kitchen
39 kitchen cabinet pull, based on the heavy/light and orthogonal/curved concept

40,41 breakfast room **42** detail of breakfast-room table

43 view of rear of house from terrace over flooded room

43

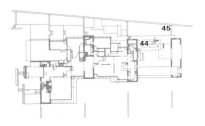

44, 45 ramp to terrace over flooded room

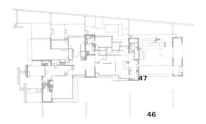

47

46

46 roof forming shade parasol

47 view of swimming pool toward flooded room

49 pool entering flooded room **50** creek entering flooded room

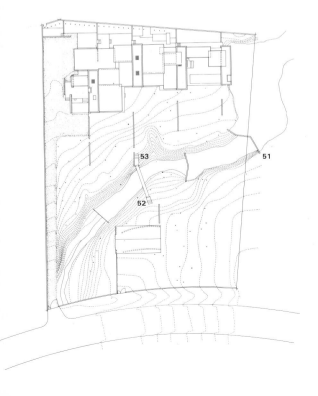

53

52

51

51 view over existing dam toward flooded
room and house (preceding pages)

52,53 bridge to guest house

54, 55 guest-house rooms facing opposite directions

Bibliography

1996

Intertwining. New York: Princeton Architectural Press, 30–43.

1995

Frampton, Kenneth. "Stretto House." *American Masterworks: The Twentieth Century House.*
New York: Rizzoli, 291–99.

Riera Ojeda, Oscar, ed. "Stretto House." *The New American House: Innovation in Residential Design and Construction.* New York: Watson-Guptill/Whitney Library of Design, 96–101.

"Steven Holl." *Architectural Design*, Jan.–Feb., 40–45.

Goldberger, Paul. "Houses as Art." *New York Times Magazine*, March 12, 54–55.

Betsky, Aaron. "De Architectuur van Steven Holl." *De Architect*, Apr., 28–49.

1994

"Architecture and Water—Steven Holl: Stretto House and Chiasma." *Architectural Design*, 40–45.

Leclerc, David. "Steven Holl: Maison a Dallas." *L'Architecture d'aujourd'hui*, Feb., 104.

Sartoris, Alberto. "Steven Holl, Stretto House." *Archithese*, Mar.–Apr., 42–44.

"A Clean Sweep." *New York Times Magazine*, April 10, 20–23.

1993

"Steven Holl." *GA Architect*, Jan., 78–89.

"Phenomenon and Idea." *Columbia University Newsline, Graduate School of Architecture, Planning and Preservation*, Mar.–Apr., 2.

Louhenjoki, Pirkko-Liisa. "Close-Up on Steven Holl." *Arkkitehti*, Apr.–May, 17–31.

"Stretto House." *GA Houses*, July 8–9, 32–59.

"Construction in Four Parts." *Lotus*, Aug., 58–67.

"Steven Holl: Espace Pensé, Espace Perçu." *Techniques et Architecture*, Oct.–Nov., 28–37.

Maunula, Leena. "Arkkitehhturria kaikille aisteille." *Helsingin Sanomat*, Nov. 27, C3.

1992

Barna, Joel Warren. "A House of Thought." *Texas Architect*, Nov., 36–37.

Barna, Joel Warren, and Michael Benedikt. "Stream & Consciousness." *Progressive Architecture*, Nov., 54–63.

Morteo, Enrico. "Stretto House." *Domus*, Dec., 56–65.

1991

Anchoring. Third edition. New York: Princeton Architectural Press, 150–56.

"Stretto House." *GA Houses*, Feb., 6–11.

Iacucci, Paola. "La Gravita e La Luce." *Phalaris*, Mar.–Apr., 32–35.

"Work in Progress." *Architectural Record*, Apr., 134–37.

1990

"House Echoes, Embraces Water." *Texas Architect*, Sept.–Oct., 44.

Photography Credits

Numbers refer to image numbers.

Paul Warchol © 1, 3, 5, 7, 8, 10, 11, 14, 18, 20, 21, 22, 27, 28, 29, 31, 36, 40, 43, 44, 45, 46, 51, 53

All other images courtesy of Steven Holl Architects.